LUXURY
of Poetry

LUXURY
of Poetry

Language as Liberation. Authority as Art.

by **Luxorae**™

Published by Luxorae™ LLC
Buffalo, New York
© 2026 Luxorae™ LLC

1st Edition
Published by:
Luxorae™ LLC
Buffalo, NY, USA
www.Luxoraelife.com

ISBN: 979-8-9947700-2-3

Printed in the United States of America

TABLE OF CONTENTS

COMPLETE GUIDE TO POETIC FORMS   60
Form as Containment, Not Constraint

THE LUXORAE POETRY PRACTICE   62
A 12-Week Liberation, Craft & Healing Curriculum

RHYTHM & PERFORMANCE GUIDE   65
The Luxorae Guide to Breath, Rhythm & Embodied Voice

CLOSING MATERIALS

DEDICATION

For every person who was told their voice was too much or not enough.
For the ancestors who spoke when speaking was dangerous.
For the lineage that survived through language.
For the griots, the preachers, the poets, the truth-tellers.
For those learning that freedom begins in the body, not in permission.

LETTER FROM THE AUTHOR

POETRY FOUND ME

I did not come to poetry because it was beautiful.

I came to it because it was honest.

Long before Luxorae had language, structure, or philosophy, I was speaking—sometimes quietly, sometimes out loud—trying to organize what I felt in a world that demanded composure without care.

Spoken word became my way of breathing in public without collapsing. It became a way to metabolize what I was carrying without turning it into spectacle.

In the Black diaspora, voice has always been communal. From griots to sermons, from chants to call-and-response, our poetry was never meant to be solitary. It was meant to circulate—to regulate the group, to hold memory, to protect dignity.

When I perform spoken word in my community, I am not performing pain.

I am practicing alignment out loud.

I chose poetry as a therapeutic modality not because it bypasses intellect, but because it integrates it. Poetry allows the nervous system to settle while truth is spoken. It allows contradiction to exist without fragmentation. It allows power to be named without domination.

Luxorae was born from this same impulse: to live without self-betrayal.

My philosophy is simple and rigorous:

Internal order precedes external authority.

Language shapes identity.

Beauty is not excess—it is coherence.

Liberation that cannot be carried internally will not last.
Poetry is how I practice that daily.
It is how I remain a voice without becoming a symbol.
It is how I stay human while holding authority.
This book is not asking you to speak for anyone.
It is inviting you to speak from yourself—clearly, calmly, and without apology.
That is not rebellion.
That is inheritance.

— **Luxorae™**

INTRODUCTION
HISTORY, FOUNDATIONS, AND ORIGINS

Luxury of Poetry reclaims poetry as a technology of liberation, internal authority, and embodied healing. Rooted in Black diasporic lineage and expressed through original Luxorae poems, this book reframes language not as decoration, but as architecture—shaping identity, regulating the nervous system, and restoring authorship of one's life.

Historical Foundations

Poetry has never been merely artistic expression for Black people—it has been survival technology. From the griots of West Africa who preserved oral histories across generations, to the spirituals that encoded escape routes and resistance messages during enslavement, to the sermon traditions that sustained hope in the face of systemic oppression, language has been our primary tool for maintaining identity, dignity, and sovereignty.

The Harlem Renaissance, the Black Arts Movement, and contemporary spoken word traditions all demonstrate how poetry functions as both individual practice and collective resistance. Writers like Langston Hughes, Gwendolyn Brooks, Audre Lorde, and Amiri Baraka didn't write poetry as decoration—they wrote it as infrastructure for maintaining internal authority when external systems denied humanity.

The Luxorae Framework

This work introduces **The Luxorae Poetics**, a framework understanding luxury as internal order, alignment as coherence between body and truth, and authority as lived rather than granted. It positions poetry as governance technology—a way to regulate the nervous system and practice sovereignty daily.

The framework emerged from a simple but profound question: What if poetry could regulate the nervous system the same way it has historically preserved culture? What if the same structures that allowed our ancestors to survive—rhythm, repetition, call-and-response, breath—could be consciously applied as therapeutic and liberatory practice?

This work is informed by neuroscience research on embodied cognition and polyvagal theory, combined with deep study of Black poetic traditions. It recognizes that **form is not restriction—it is containment**. The same way a sonnet's structure creates space for complexity, the same way a villanelle's repetition allows processing without overwhelm, poetic form can stabilize what feeling alone cannot hold.

Who This Book Serves

From this foundation, Luxorae enters into poetic conversation with influential Black writers—including James Baldwin, Langston Hughes, Gwendolyn Brooks, Audre Lorde, Claudia Rankine, June Jordan, Lucille Clifton, Amiri Baraka, Sterling A. Brown, Claude McKay, Sonia Sanchez, Nikki Giovanni, Maya Angelou, and Toni Morrison—honoring their lineage while extending their insights into a contemporary practice of embodied authorship.

Each lineage chapter follows a consistent, practice-oriented structure: a Luxorae principle, historical grounding, an original conversation poem, guided writing prompts, a regulation practice, and key conceptual terms.

This format ensures the work remains accessible to readers without formal literary training while offering depth for scholars, writers, and educators.

The Practice at the Core

At the heart of the book is **The Luxorae Poetry Practice**, a 12-week liberation, craft, and healing curriculum that guides readers from expression to alignment. Drawing on neuroscience-informed regulation, poetic form, breath, rhythm, and reflective inquiry, the practice helps readers write without self-erasure, regulate emotion through language, and develop a stable, sovereign voice. The curriculum is designed to be lived slowly, individually or in community, and functions as both a creative practice and a therapeutic modality.

The Complete Forms Guide

Luxury of Poetry also includes **The Complete Guide to Poetic Forms**—a comprehensive reference covering sonnet, haiku, villanelle, pantoum, sestina, ghazal, free verse, prose poetry, lyric, spoken word, blues poetry, and vernacular traditions—framing form as containment rather than constraint. Each form is explained with historical context, structural requirements, contemporary examples, and writing exercises.

What This Book Is Not

This book is not a manifesto, nor a self-help text. It does not assign saviorhood or promise transformation. It does not appropriate traditional forms or claim to speak for all Black experiences. Instead, it offers a grounded, repeatable practice for readers seeking clarity without collapse, voice without performance, and liberation without self-betrayal.

Luxury of Poetry is written for poets and non-poets alike—for anyone ready to experience language as a site of freedom, coherence, and inheritance lived.

MANIFESTO:
WHY POETRY. WHY NOW.

A Statement of Purpose and Practice

Poetry was never decoration for our people.
It was survival compressed into breath.

Before we had land, we had language.
Before we had safety, we had rhythm.
Before we had permission, we had voice.

This book exists because poetry has been misframed—as art without consequence, expression without structure, emotion without authority. But for Black people across the diaspora, poetry has always been a **technology of liberation**, a method of internal governance, and a way to remain whole when the external world demanded fragmentation. From griots to spirituals, from coded sermons to spoken word stages, poetry has been how we told the truth when the truth could not be spoken plainly.

This is not a book about writing beautifully.
It is a book about writing truthfully without collapse.

From a Luxorae perspective, poetry is luxury—not because it is rarefied, but because it creates **space**. Space to breathe. Space to feel. Space to regulate. Space to remember who you are without urgency.

Poetry slows the nervous system.
Form restores order.
Voice reclaims authorship.

This book invites you not to perform pain, but to reorganize it.
Not to relive trauma, but to contain it.
Not to chase healing, but to practice alignment.

Poetry is not an escape.
It is a return.

HOW TO USE THIS BOOK

This book is designed to be experienced in multiple ways:
- **As a solo journey** — Work through it at your own pace, using the prompts and practices for personal reflection and writing.
- **As a community practice** — Gather with others to read, write, and witness together. The call-and-response structure supports group work.
- **As an educational text** — Use it in classrooms, workshops, or therapeutic settings to teach both craft and embodied voice.
- **As a reference guide** — Return to specific chapters, forms, or lineage conversations as needed.

Structure:
- **Part I** introduces Voice Before Permission—the foundational claim to self through language.
- **Part II** explores Form as Containment—how structure holds what feeling cannot.
- **Part III** examines Language as Liberation—truth without collapse.
- **Part IV** cultivates Sovereign Speech—voice after alignment.
- **Part V** honors Inheritance Lived—poetry as continuity and legacy.

Each chapter includes: a Luxorae principle, original poem, historical context, guided prompts, regulation practice, and key terms.

You do not need to read this book in order. Follow what calls to you. Return to what serves you. Skip what doesn't resonate yet—it may later.

A NOTE ON LINEAGE AND DIASPORA

The writers honored in this book—James Baldwin, Langston Hughes, Gwendolyn Brooks, Audre Lorde, Claudia Rankine, June Jordan, Lucille Clifton, Amiri Baraka, Sterling A. Brown, Claude McKay, Sonia Sanchez, Nikki Giovanni, Maya Angelou, and Toni Morrison—are not presented as heroes to worship or icons to analyze from a distance.

They are presented as **architects**—people who built internal authority under external constraint.

Each conversation poem in this book is not imitation, nor biography. It is **dialogue across time**—a way of honoring lineage by extending it, not freezing it.

The diaspora did not only survive through labor and endurance; it survived through **language technologies**: spirituals, sermons, call-and-response, praise, coded speech, testimony, rhythm.

This book positions poetry as one of those technologies—refined, repeatable, and alive.

Luxorae does not approach these writers as 'inspiration.' Luxorae approaches them as people who built **internal sovereignty** when the world denied external freedom.

IN CONVERSATION WITH AUDRE LORDE: REDEFINING LUXURY

This book's title, *Luxury of Poetry*, is in direct conversation with Audre Lorde's 1980 essay "Poetry Is Not a Luxury."

At first glance, these titles appear contradictory:

Audre Lorde (1980): "Poetry is **NOT** a luxury"

Luxorae (2026): "**Luxury** of Poetry"

But this is only a surface tension. When examined deeply, these works are **in conversation, not opposition**—they complete each other across 46 years.

What Audre Lorde Meant by "NOT a Luxury"

Lorde was writing in 1980, against a specific cultural moment where poetry was seen as **frivolous**, decorative, non-essential. "Real work" meant political organizing, economic survival. The arts were considered **indulgent** compared to "serious" activism. Women's interior lives were dismissed as trivial. Black women's feelings were deemed irrelevant to liberation.

Lorde argued that poetry is **not a luxury** in the sense that it is:

- **NOT optional** for survival
- **NOT decorative** or ornamental
- **NOT frivolous** compared to "real work"
- **NOT separate** from political action
- **NOT indulgent**—it is **essential**

She wrote:

"For women, then, poetry is not a luxury. It is a vital necessity of our existence. It forms the quality of the light within which we predicate our hopes and dreams toward survival and change, first made into language, then into idea, then into more tangible action."

For Lorde, "luxury" meant **unnecessary excess, privilege, frivolity, something you can do without.**

She was reclaiming poetry as **infrastructure, not decoration.**

What Luxorae Means by "Luxury of Poetry"

Luxorae is writing in 2026, in a moment where:

- Poetry has been **weaponized** as trauma performance
- Vulnerability has become **currency** in late-stage capitalism
- "Hustle culture" demands constant productivity, including from artists
- Self-exploitation is rebranded as "authenticity"
- Rest, space, and boundaries are still seen as **selfish**
- Black women are still expected to **collapse** to prove legitimacy

Luxorae argues that poetry is a **luxury** in the sense that it is:

- **Space** to breathe without urgency
- **Permission** to feel without performing
- **Internal order** that doesn't leak or press
- **Sovereignty** practiced without external validation
- **Alignment** between body and truth
- **Coherence** that requires no self-erasure

In the *Luxury of Poetry* framework, "luxury" = **internal order, spaciousness, freedom from urgency, no self-betrayal, what does not press or leak.**

Luxorae is reclaiming **luxury itself**—redefining it as internal order, not external excess.

The Redefinition of "Luxury"
Both Lorde and Luxorae reject poetry as decorative, frivolous, non-essential, performative, or separate from survival.

What Lorde Reclaimed:
Poetry as **essential, necessary, vital, foundational**—the opposite of luxury-as-frivolity.

What Luxorae Reclaims:
Luxury itself—redefining it as **internal spaciousness, sovereignty, alignment, coherence**—the very thing Lorde said poetry provides.

The Shared Foundation
Both Lorde and Luxorae argue:

- ☑ **Poetry is survival technology**
- ☑ **Poetry is not performance**
- ☑ **Poetry creates internal authority**
- ☑ **Poetry allows self-definition**
- ☑ **Poetry is political**
- ☑ **Poetry is necessary, not optional**

The Key Difference

Lorde's Urgency:
Poetry is **necessary** because without it, we cannot survive, cannot name ourselves, cannot act.
Energy: Insistence, defense, declaration
Context: Fighting to legitimize poetry as essential work
Message: "This matters. This is not frivolous. This is necessary."

Luxorae's Sovereignty:

Poetry is **luxury** because it allows us to exist with spaciousness, alignment, and internal order—without urgency, performance, or self-erasure.

Energy: Groundedness, calm authority, occupancy

Context: Moving beyond survival into sustainable sovereignty

Message: "I am not performing necessity. I am practicing luxury as internal freedom."

The Generational Shift

Lorde (1980): Poetry as Legitimacy

"I must prove poetry is not frivolous. I must defend its necessity."

Luxorae (2026): Poetry as Sovereignty

"I do not need to defend poetry. I practice it as internal order. That is luxury."

This is not rejection—it is evolution.

Lorde had to **fight for poetry to be seen as essential**.

Luxorae can now **practice poetry as sovereignty** because Lorde won that fight.

Where They Meet: The Erotic

Lorde's essay "Poetry Is Not a Luxury" is companion to her essay "Uses of the Erotic: The Erotic as Power."

In both, she argues:

- Depth is intelligence
- Feeling is not frivolous
- Internal knowing precedes external action
- What we've been taught to dismiss is actually essential

Luxorae directly inherits this:

- **Source** (Luxorae term) = **The Erotic** (Lorde's term)
- Both mean: life-force intelligence, what knows before proof, embodied truth

They're saying the same thing in different language for different moments.

The Synthesis

If we place these works in conversation:

Lorde says: Poetry is not a luxury—it is necessary.

Luxorae says: Yes. And necessity practiced with sovereignty **is** luxury.

Lorde says: Poetry is the skeleton architecture of our lives.

Luxorae says: Yes. And that architecture, when it holds us without pressing, is luxury.

Lorde says: Poetry is the quality of light by which we scrutinize our lives.

Luxorae says: Yes. And that light, when it does not demand performance, is luxury.

Why "Luxury of Poetry" Honors Lorde

Luxorae is not contradicting Lorde.

Luxorae is **completing** Lorde's work.

Lorde fought to prove poetry was essential.

Luxorae practices it as sovereignty.

Lorde said: "This is not frivolous."

Luxorae says: "And because it's not frivolous, it is luxury—true luxury, which is internal freedom."

Lorde gave us permission to take poetry seriously.

Luxorae gives us permission to practice it with ease.

The Final Word

Audre Lorde (1980):

"Poetry is not a luxury. It is a vital necessity of our existence."

Luxorae (2026):

"Poetry is luxury. Not because it is excess, but because it is the only thing that allows us to exist without collapse. Luxury is not what shines. It is what does not press."

Together:
Poetry is necessary (Lorde).
Necessity practiced with sovereignty is luxury (Luxury of poetry).
Both are true.

This is not contradiction.
This is lineage.

BLACK POETRY AS LIBERATION TECHNOLOGY: A TIMELINE

1700s — SURVIVAL THROUGH VERSE
1773 — Phillis Wheatley publishes *Poems on Various Subjects, Religious and Moral*, becoming the first published African American poet. Her work proves Black intellectual capacity in a world denying Black humanity.

Key Insight: Poetry as proof of personhood when the law denied it.

1800s — CODED LANGUAGE & RESISTANCE
1845 — Frederick Douglass publishes his narrative, using literary form to argue for abolition.
1850s-1865 — Spirituals function as coded communication, with songs like "Follow the Drinking Gourd" providing escape routes via the Underground Railroad.
1892 — Frances Ellen Watkins Harper publishes *Iola Leroy*, combining poetry and prose to address racial injustice.
Key Insight: Poetry as encrypted resistance and survival strategy.

1900s-1920s — THE NEW NEGRO MOVEMENT
1903 — Paul Laurence Dunbar's dialectic poetry honors Black vernacular as legitimate literary language.

1920s-1930s — THE HARLEM RENAISSANCE

- Langston Hughes: *The Weary Blues* (1926) — Jazz poetry, ordinary Black life as worthy subject
- Claude McKay: *Harlem Shadows* (1922) — Rage contained in sonnet form
- Countee Cullen: *Color* (1925) — Formal mastery meets racial consciousness
- Zora Neale Hurston: Preserves oral traditions and folklore

Key Insight: Poetry as cultural reclamation and identity assertion.

1940s-1950s — QUIET REVOLUTION

1945 — Gwendolyn Brooks publishes *A Street in Bronzeville*, dignifying Black interior life.

1950 — Brooks wins Pulitzer Prize for *Annie Allen* — first African American to receive it.

Key Insight: Poetry proving that the personal is political, that home is sovereignty.

1960s-1970s — THE BLACK ARTS MOVEMENT

1960s — BLACK ARTS MOVEMENT (the artistic arm of Black Power)

- Amiri Baraka (LeRoi Jones): Revolutionary poetry as political action
- Nikki Giovanni: Black joy and love as resistance
- Sonia Sanchez: Blending spirituality, politics, and breath
- The Last Poets: Spoken word as communal practice
- Audre Lorde: *The First Cities* (1968) — Poetry as survival necessity

1970 — Maya Angelou publishes *I Know Why the Caged Bird Sings*

Key Insight: Poetry as weapon, ritual, and community-building tool.

1980s-1990s — EXPANSION & DIVERSIFICATION

1980 — Audre Lorde: "Poetry is Not a Luxury" essay — redefining poetry as essential, not decorative

1987 — Toni Morrison wins Pulitzer for *Beloved*

1990s — SPOKEN WORD RENAISSANCE

- Nuyorican Poets Cafe becomes epicenter of performance poetry
- Def Poetry Jam brings spoken word to mainstream (2002-2007)
- Slam poetry movement democratizes poetic practice
- Hip-hop as poetic form gains academic recognition

Key Insight: Poetry returns to oral roots; performance as embodied practice.

2000s — CONTEMPORARY VOICES

2000s-Present:

- Claudia Rankine: *Citizen: An American Lyric* (2014) — Prose poetry documenting microaggressions
- Danez Smith: Gender, Blackness, and survival
- Jericho Brown: *The Tradition* (2019) — Pulitzer Prize
- Amanda Gorman: "The Hill We Climb" (2021) — youngest inaugural poet
- Ocean Vuong: Hybrid forms and diaspora memory
- Terrance Hayes: Golden Shovel form innovation

Key Insight: Poetry as healing modality, nervous system regulation, and contemporary resistance.

PRESENT DAY — POETRY AS HEALING TECHNOLOGY

2020s:

- Poetry therapy recognized in clinical settings
- Neuroscience research on rhythm and nervous system regulation
- Social media democratizes poetry distribution
- Poetry as tool for processing collective trauma (pandemic, racial violence, political upheaval)

- **The Luxorae Framework**: Poetry as governance technology, internal sovereignty practice

Key Insight: Poetry comes full circle — from survival to liberation to regulation to sovereignty.

CORE THREAD ACROSS TIME:

Poetry has always been how Black people:

- **Preserved** identity when systems tried to erase it
- **Encoded** resistance when direct speech was dangerous
- **Regulated** the body when the world demanded collapse
- **Claimed** authority before it was granted
- **Built** worlds when the existing one denied humanity

Poetry is not art for us. It is infrastructure.

THE LUXORAE POETICS

Language as Liberation. Form as Authority.

The Luxorae Poetics is a framework for understanding poetry not as creative expression, but as **governance technology**—a way to regulate the nervous system, reclaim authorship, and practice sovereignty daily.

Core Principles:

1. **Luxury is internal order.**
   It is not what shines. It is what does not press, leak, or require self-erasure.

2. **Alignment is coherence.**
   It is the match between inner truth and outer life, between body and language, between what you feel and what you speak.

3. Authority is lived, not granted.

You do not wait for permission to speak from yourself. You practice it until it becomes your resting state.

4. Form is containment, not constraint.

Structure creates safety for the nervous system. It allows emotion to be felt without fragmentation.

5. Voice precedes access.

Before rights, before recognition, before approval—voice exists. Poetry trains you to trust it.

6. Liberation that cannot be carried internally will not last.

Freedom is not only systemic—it is practiced in how you speak, breathe, and organize yourself daily.

Luxorae Key Terms:

- **Authorship** — Choosing yourself without negotiation
- **Alignment** — Inner truth matching outer life
- **Luxury** — No self-erasure required for peace
- **Coherence** — Body and truth agreeing
- **Sovereignty** — Internal governance without external validation
- **Source** — Life-force intelligence; what knows before proof
- **Occupancy** — Presence without urgency; fullness without performance

PART I — VOICE BEFORE PERMISSION

"I am not tragically colored. There is no great sorrow dammed up in my soul, nor lurking behind my eyes... Even in the helter-skelter skirmish that is my life, I have seen that the world is to the strong regardless of a little pigmentation more or less."

— Zora Neale Hurston

PART I INTRODUCTION
Poetry as the First Claim to Self

Before Black people were granted rights, we still spoke.
Before we were allowed literacy, we still named ourselves.
Before we were treated as human, we still carried meaning.
That is the first logic of this book: voice precedes access.
Institutions often treat poetry as art. For us, poetry has been **infrastructure**—a way to preserve identity when systems tried to rewrite it. The diaspora did not only survive through labor and endurance; it survived through language technologies: spirituals, sermons, call-and-response, praise, coded speech, testimony, rhythm.
This section begins with voice because sovereignty begins there.
A person who cannot speak from themselves will always be governed by what others call them.
Luxorae does not approach these writers as "inspiration." Luxorae approaches them as architects—people who built internal authority under external constraint.
Each poem that follows is a conversation: not imitation, not biography—a dialogue across time. After each piece, you will find prompts designed for solo journaling or facilitated circles. The goal is not analysis. The goal is alignment.

CHAPTER 1
BEFORE I WAS ALLOWED

Language as Survival
Form Focus: Free Verse

Luxorae Principle

Voice does not require permission. It exists before approval, before literacy, before anyone calls it valid. The first revolutionary act is speaking from yourself.

Original Luxorae Poem

I learned early
that silence was safer
than precision.
That truth could live in my chest
as long as it did not ask for air.
But the body does not forget
what it was forced to hold.
Every unspoken sentence
waited for me
like inheritance.

Understanding Free Verse

Free verse is poetry without fixed meter or rhyme scheme. It allows the writer to organize language according to breath, thought, and emphasis rather than predetermined rules.

Key Elements:
- Line breaks create meaning and rhythm
- Whitespace functions as silence or pause
- Natural speech patterns guide the form
- Repetition and imagery carry emotional weight

Free verse is often where beginning poets start because it feels accessible. But freedom without intention becomes formlessness. The discipline of free verse is **choosing where to break the line**—and that choice shapes how the reader experiences the poem.

Guided Writing Prompts
1. Write a poem beginning: "I learned early..." What did you learn before you were taught?
2. What truth have you held in your chest without speaking it? Write it now.
3. Where have you mistaken silence for safety? Write about a moment you chose voice instead.
4. Complete this sentence ten times: "Before I was allowed, I..."

Regulation Practice

Voice Grounding Exercise:
Sit comfortably. Place one hand on your chest.
Speak one true sentence aloud. It can be simple: "I am here." "I exist." "This is my voice."
Notice how your body responds to hearing your own voice claim truth.
Repeat daily for seven days.

Key Terms
- **Authorship**: The practice of naming yourself
- **Voice**: Internal truth made audible
- **Sovereignty**: Speaking from yourself without waiting for permission

CHAPTER 2
THE MOUTH REMEMBERS

Orality, Rhythm, and Diaspora Memory
Form Focus: Spoken Word / Griot Lineage

Luxorae Principle

Before written language, we had oral tradition. The mouth remembers what paper cannot hold—rhythm, tone, breath, call-and-response. Spoken word is not performance; it is embodied memory practiced aloud.

Original Luxorae Poem

Before paper,
we trusted breath.
Before approval,
we trusted rhythm.
What I speak now
has passed through
many mouths—
none of them owned,
all of them sovereign.

Understanding Spoken Word

Spoken word poetry centers oral delivery. It prioritizes rhythm, breath, repetition, and audience engagement.

Key elements:
- Natural speech patterns
- Intentional pauses
- Vocal dynamics
- Call-and-response structure

This form connects directly to griot traditions, Black sermon culture, and diaspora storytelling—where voice carries history forward.

Guided Writing Prompts
1. Write a poem using the phrase "Before..." at the start of each stanza.
2. What rhythm lives in your body? Write to that pulse.
3. Complete: "My mouth remembers..." Write what your body knows without proof.
4. Write a poem meant to be read aloud. How does sound change meaning?

Regulation Practice

Breath & Rhythm Exercise:
Tap your heartbeat for 30 seconds. Write to that rhythm.
Read your poem aloud three times, adjusting line breaks to match your natural breath.
Notice where you pause.

Key Terms
- **Orality**: Knowledge carried through voice, not text
- **Rhythm**: The body's natural pulse informing language
- **Diaspora Memory**: Inherited knowing across generations

CHAPTER 3

WHAT WAS NEVER SILENT

Ancestral Voice and Inherited Knowing
Form Focus: Praise Poetry

Luxorae Principle

Praise is not flattery. It is recognition of what endures. Ancestral voice speaks through lineage—honoring those who built internal sovereignty when external freedom was denied.

Original Luxorae Poem

Praise the women
who knew before knowing
had a name.
Praise the men
who carried dignity
without witnesses.
Praise the children
who learned quiet
was not emptiness
but listening.

Understanding Praise Poetry

Praise poetry honors what survives. It names strength without sentimentality, dignity without approval.

Key elements:

- Direct naming
- Repetition for emphasis
- Acknowledgment of what endures

This form connects to African praise songs, testaments, and acknowledgment traditions—where naming creates presence.

Guided Writing Prompts

1. Write a praise poem for yourself without irony or diminishment.
2. Praise someone who was never publicly recognized. What did they preserve?
3. Complete: "Praise..." ten times. Name what you inherited that you did not choose.
4. What ancestor do you carry in your voice?

Regulation Practice

Ancestral Acknowledgment:

Light a candle. Speak aloud one quality you inherited from your lineage. Say it three times.
Notice what shifts in your body.

Key Terms

- **Praise**: Recognition without flattery
- **Ancestral Voice**: Inherited knowing across time
- **Lineage**: Connection to those who came before

PART II — FORM AS CONTAINMENT

"We have to confront ourselves. Do we like what we see in the mirror? And, according to our light, according to our understanding, according to our courage, we will have to say yea or nay—and rise!"

— Maya Angelou

PART II INTRODUCTION

Discipline Is Not Oppression

Form is not restriction. It is the container that allows feeling to be held without fragmentation. Structure creates safety for the nervous system—it lets emotion exist without overwhelming the body.

This section explores how traditional poetic forms (sonnet, villanelle, haiku) function as governance tools—ways to regulate intensity, process repetition, and practice precision.

When form is understood as **containment rather than constraint**, it becomes liberatory.

The same structures that have existed for centuries—14 lines, repeating refrains, syllable counts—are not arbitrary rules. They are **nervous system architecture**. They allow the brain to predict, to process, to integrate.

A sonnet's volta (turn) creates space for shift.

A villanelle's repetition allows trauma to be metabolized.

A haiku's brevity forces precision that reduces overwhelm.

Form is mercy.

CHAPTER 4
STRUCTURE HOLDS WHAT FEELING CANNOT

Why Form Heals
Form Focus: Sonnet

Luxorae Principle

Restraint is not another cage. Form became the place I laid what grief could not afford to sprawl. Within these lines, my breath returned.

Original Luxorae Poem (Sonnet)

I thought restraint was another cage,
another rule disguised as moral law.
But form became the place I laid
what grief could not afford to sprawl.
Within these lines, my breath returned.
No panic leaked beyond the frame.
I learned: containment is not earned—
it is the nervous system's name.
What broke me was not discipline,
but living without any edge.
Now structure holds what pain was in
and keeps my center from the ledge.
I am not smaller in this form.
I am finally warm.

Understanding the Sonnet

A sonnet is 14 lines with a specific rhyme scheme.

Shakespearean Sonnet: ABABCDCDEFEFGG

Petrarchan Sonnet: ABBAABBA CDECDE (or CDCDCD)

The structure creates natural turns—places where thought shifts. The **volta** (turn) typically happens at line 9 in Petrarchan sonnets, or in the final couplet in Shakespearean sonnets.

The form's restraint allows complex emotion to be held without chaos.

Why it works:

- Predictable structure = nervous system safety
- Limited scope (14 lines) = manageable emotional container
- Rhyme scheme = rhythmic regulation
- Volta = space for shift, resolution, or deepening

Guided Writing Prompts

1. Write about a time structure saved you. Use 14 lines.
2. What emotion needs containment? Place it inside a sonnet's frame.
3. Identify the "turn" (volta) in your own life. Where did something shift?
4. Write a sonnet where the final couplet contradicts the previous 12 lines.

Regulation Practice

Container Breath:

Inhale for 4 counts, hold for 4, exhale for 4, hold for 4.

Repeat 14 times (one per line of a sonnet).

Notice how counting contains the breath.

Key Terms

- **Containment**: Structure that holds without crushing
- **Form**: The shape that allows feeling to exist safely
- **Volta**: The turn; where meaning shifts

CHAPTER 5
REPETITION IS A TEACHER

Cycles, Trauma, and Return
Form Focus: Villanelle

Luxorae Principle

We repeat what we have not metabolized. The villanelle teaches that repetition is not failure—it is the way the mind processes what it cannot hold all at once.

Original Luxorae Poem (Villanelle excerpt)

I learned to leave before I stayed.
I learned to brace before the calm.
I learned to leave before I stayed.
Each promise dressed itself as aid,
each love arrived with hidden harm.
I learned to leave before I stayed.
Until the pattern named the trade:
escape disguised as wisdom's balm.
I learned to leave before I stayed—
and then I didn't.
That's how it changed.

Understanding the Villanelle

A villanelle is a 19-line poem with two repeating refrains.

Structure:
- 5 tercets (3-line stanzas) + 1 quatrain (4-line stanza)
- Line 1 repeats in lines 6, 12, 18
- Line 3 repeats in lines 9, 15, 19
- Rhyme scheme: ABA ABA ABA ABA ABA ABAA

The repetition is not monotony—it's how **trauma processes**. Each return to the refrain allows new meaning to emerge.

Why it works:
- Repetition desensitizes emotional charge
- Each cycle allows deeper integration
- The brain processes in layers; repetition creates space for that
- Final quatrain brings both refrains together = resolution

Guided Writing Prompts
1. What pattern do you keep repeating? Write it as a refrain.
2. Write the same line three times. What changes each time you return to it?
3. Identify one inherited belief. Write it into a villanelle's repetition.
4. Where did a cycle finally break for you? Write that as the final stanza.

Regulation Practice

Pattern Recognition:
Identify one pattern you repeat (in relationships, work, self-talk).
Say it aloud three times, noticing what shifts in your body each time.
By the third time, does it feel different?

Key Terms
- **Repetition**: The mind's way of processing
- **Cycle**: Return that allows integration
- **Pattern**: What we repeat until we metabolize it

CHAPTER 6

WHEN LESS IS ENOUGH

Breath, Presence, and Precision
Form Focus: Haiku & Tanka

Luxorae Principle

Luxury is not excess. It is having exactly what you need. Haiku teaches precision—saying everything in the fewest words possible.

Original Luxorae Poem (Haiku)

No one applauds
the moment I choose rest—
still, the room shifts.

Understanding Haiku

Haiku: 3 lines (5-7-5 syllables traditionally, though contemporary haiku often breaks this)

Captures a single moment.

Key elements:

- Present-tense observation
- Natural imagery
- Implied emotion (not stated directly)
- A "cutting" moment—juxtaposition of two images

Tanka: 5 lines (5-7-5-7-7 syllables)
Extends haiku by adding reflection or emotional depth.
The form teaches **restraint and presence**.

Why it works:
- Brevity reduces overwhelm
- Forces writer to distill to essence
- Single focus = grounded attention
- No room for explanation = pure observation

Guided Writing Prompts
1. Write a haiku about a moment no one witnessed.
2. What needs fewer words? Reduce a paragraph to 3 lines.
3. Write 5 haiku in one sitting. Notice which one feels most true.
4. Expand one haiku into a tanka. What does the extra space allow?

Regulation Practice

Minimalist Pause:
Remove one unnecessary thing from your day (an obligation, a commitment, an item).
Notice the space it creates.

Key Terms
- **Precision**: Saying everything with less
- **Restraint**: Choosing what to leave out
- **Essence**: What remains when excess is removed

PART III — LANGUAGE AS LIBERATION

"The most common way people give up their power is by thinking they don't have any."

— Alice Walker

PART III INTRODUCTION

Truth Without Collapse

Liberation is not loudness.

Liberation is truth that does not require you to break yourself to be believed.

This section explores how language becomes liberation when it:

- Names what was unnamed
- Refuses what was imposed
- Trusts what the body knows

Rage does not have to burn you.

Erasure can reclaim authority.

The body speaks before the mind translates.

Language as liberation means: **speaking truth without collapsing under its weight**.

CHAPTER 7
ANGER WITHOUT FIRE

Rage That Does Not Burn the Body
Form Focus: Controlled Free Verse

Luxorae Principle

I do not raise my voice because my truth does not require oxygen theft. Anger, held properly, is clarity—not combustion.

Original Luxorae Poem

I do not raise my voice
because my truth
does not require oxygen theft.
Anger, held properly,
is clarity—
not combustion.
I refuse to burn
what I am trying
to protect.

Guided Writing Prompts

1. Write anger inside strict line breaks. Don't let it sprawl.
2. Where does your rage point? What is it protecting?
3. Complete: "I am done pretending..."
4. Write rage as information, not explosion.

Regulation Practice

Pacing Practice:

When anger arises, pause for 30 seconds before speaking or writing. Let the intensity settle into clarity.

Key Terms
- **Clarity**: Anger without chaos
- **Containment**: Holding rage without burning

CHAPTER 8
ERASING THE LAW

Reclaiming Authority from Imposed Texts
Form Focus: Erasure Poetry

Luxorae Principle

Not all language is mine. Some was imposed. Erasure reclaims authority by removing what does not belong.

Original Luxorae Poem (Conceptual Erasure)

I was taught
to wait
to submit
to endure
—until I wasn't.

Guided Writing Prompts

1. Take a text that once governed you (a rule, a policy, a religious text, a contract). Erase until only your truth remains.
2. What law would you erase?
3. Write about authority you refuse.

Regulation Practice

Editing Practice:

Remove one rule you've been following that you never agreed to.

Key Terms

- **Erasure**: Removing what was imposed
- **Authority**: Reclaiming what is yours

CHAPTER 9
WHAT THE BODY KNOWS

The Nervous System Speaks
Form Focus: Lyric Prose

Luxorae Principle

The body speaks in temperature, not sentences. It tightens when a lie approaches. It exhales when alignment arrives.

Original Luxorae Poem (Lyric Prose)

The body speaks in temperature, not sentences.
It tightens when a lie approaches.
It exhales when alignment arrives.
I stopped asking my body to cooperate with my fear.
Now it cooperates with my truth.

Guided Writing Prompts

1. Write from sensation, not story. What does your body know?
2. Where does anxiety live in your body? Describe its shape.
3. Complete: "My body knows..."

Regulation Practice

Body Scan:

Name sensation without story for 2 minutes.

Key Terms

- **Embodiment**: Trusting the body's knowing
- **Sensation**: Information before interpretation

PART IV — SOVEREIGN SPEECH

"I am deliberate and afraid of nothing."

— Audre Lorde

PART IV INTRODUCTION

Voice After Alignment

Sovereignty is not loud.
It does not argue.
It does not perform.
It stands.
This section explores voice after alignment—when you no longer need to convince anyone, including yourself.

CHAPTER 10
I DO NOT EXPLAIN MYSELF

Boundaries as Poetry
Form Focus: Epigram & Aphorism

Luxorae Principle
Clarity does not argue. It stands.

Original Luxorae Poem (Epigram)
Clarity does not argue.
It stands.

Guided Writing Prompts
1. Write ten one-sentence truths you no longer negotiate.
2. What boundary needs no explanation?
3. Practice saying no in 3 words or fewer.

Regulation Practice

Boundary Statement:
Speak aloud: "I do not explain myself when..."
Complete it. Mean it.

Key Terms
- **Clarity**: Truth without justification
- **Boundary**: What requires no explanation

CHAPTER 11
CALL AND RESPONSE

Community, Witness, Circulation
Form Focus: Call-and-Response Poem

Luxorae Principle

Voice is not only individual. It circulates. Call-and-response is co-regulation made audible.

Original Luxorae Poem

Call: Who governs you?
Response: I do.
Call: Who decides your pace?
Response: I do.
Call: Who benefits from your silence?
Response: Not anymore.

Guided Writing Prompts

1. Write a call-and-response meant to be read aloud with others.
2. What question do you need the community to answer with you?

Regulation Practice

Community Witnessing:
Share one poem with a trusted person. No feedback required—just witnessing.

Key Terms
- **Co-Regulation**: Shared nervous system safety
- **Witnessing**: Being heard without judgment

CHAPTER 12
THE QUIET AFTER POWER

What Remains When Nothing Is Leaking
Form Focus: Open Choice

Luxorae Principle

Nothing rushes here. Nothing proves itself. Nothing leaks. This is not emptiness. This is occupancy.

Original Luxorae Poem

Nothing rushes here.
Nothing proves itself.
Nothing leaks.
This is not emptiness.
This is occupancy.

Guided Writing Prompts

1. Write a poem that doesn't try to convince anyone of anything.
2. What does occupancy feel like in your body?

Regulation Practice

Stillness Practice:

Sit for 5 minutes without doing anything.
Notice the difference between emptiness and fullness.

Key Terms

- **Occupancy**: Presence without urgency
- **Stillness**: Power at rest

PART V — INHERITANCE LIVED

"If you surrendered to the air, you could ride it."

— Toni Morrison

PART V INTRODUCTION

Poetry as Continuity

This section is about legacy.
Not legacy as what you leave behind when you die.
Legacy as what you practice while you live.
Inheritance lived means:

- Integration over performance
- Space over urgency
- Wholeness over perfection

CHAPTER 13
NOT PERFECT, BUT WHOLE

Integration Over Performance
Form Focus: Hybrid Form

Luxorae Principle

I am not flawless. I am integrated. The war ended when I stopped fighting myself for existing honestly.

Original Luxorae Poem

I am not flawless.
I am integrated.
The war ended
when I stopped
fighting myself
for existing honestly.

Guided Writing Prompts

1. What are you integrating that you used to reject?
2. Write about the moment you chose yourself.

Regulation Practice

Integration Statement:

"I am not broken. I am..."
Complete it.

Key Terms

- **Integration**: Wholeness, not perfection
- **Coherence**: All parts agreeing

CHAPTER 14
LUXURY IS SPACE

Ease, Margin, and Time
Form Focus: Minimalist Poem

Luxorae Principle
Luxury is not what shines. It is what does not press.

Original Luxorae Poem
Luxury
is not what shines.
It is what does not press.

Guided Writing Prompts
1. What would your life look like with more space?
2. Where can you remove excess?

Regulation Practice

Space Practice:
Create one hour of unscheduled time this week.
Do nothing.

Key Terms
- **Luxury**: Internal spaciousness
- **Margin**: Room to breathe

CHAPTER 15

WHAT WE LEAVE INTACT

Poetry as Legacy
Form Focus: Letter Poem

Luxorae Principle
Legacy is not what you achieve. It is what you leave intact.

Original Luxorae Poem (Letter Poem)
To whoever comes after me—
May you inherit ease,
not urgency.
May you trust your voice
before you are told it matters.
May nothing in you
need to break
to be believed.

Guided Writing Prompts
1. Write a letter poem to your future self.
2. Write a letter poem to the next generation.
3. What do you want to leave intact?

Regulation Practice

Legacy Statement:
Complete: "I want to be remembered for..."
Then ask: "Am I living that now?"

Key Terms

- **Legacy**: What you practice, not what you achieve
- **Inheritance**: What you pass forward

THE LUXORAE PROMPT LIBRARY
75 Writing Exercises Organized by Theme

VOICE RECLAMATION PROMPTS

1. Complete this line 10 times: "Before I was told to be quiet, I..."
2. Write about the first time you silenced yourself. What did you lose?
3. "My voice sounds like..." — Describe your voice without judgment.
4. Write a poem titled "Permission Denied"
5. What would you say if no one could interrupt you?
6. List 10 things you've never said aloud. Choose one. Write it.
7. "I speak from..." — Where does your voice originate in your body?
8. Write about a time someone tried to speak for you.
9. Complete: "My truth is not up for debate when..."
10. Write a poem using only statements, no questions.

ANCESTRAL MEMORY PROMPTS

11. What did your grandmother's hands know that yours forgot?
12. Write from the voice of an ancestor you never met.
13. "I inherited..." — Name 5 things (not objects).
14. What rhythm lives in your bloodline?
15. Write about a food that carries memory.
16. Complete: "My people survived by..."
17. What language did your ancestors speak? Write in that energy.
18. List the names you were almost called. Why does your name matter?

19. Write a praise poem for someone in your lineage who was never celebrated.
20. "Before this country, my people..." — Finish the sentence 5 ways.

RAGE & RELEASE PROMPTS

21. Write about anger without using the word "angry."
22. What would you burn if fire couldn't hurt you?
23. Complete: "I am done pretending..."
24. Write a list of everything you're not apologizing for anymore.
25. "They taught me to be small. I choose..."
26. Write about rage that doesn't destroy you.
27. What boundary would you draw in blood?
28. Write the letter you'll never send. Then erase half of it.
29. "No" is a complete sentence. Write 10 variations of it.
30. What are you protecting by staying silent?

JOY & PLEASURE PROMPTS

31. Write about pleasure without justifying it.
32. List 20 things that make you feel alive.
33. "I allow myself..." — Complete 10 times.
34. What does your body want that your mind denies?
35. Write about rest as resistance.
36. Describe luxury in 3 lines.
37. What brings you joy that others don't understand?
38. Write a love letter to your own body.
39. "I deserve..." — Say it 15 times. Mean it.
40. What would delight look like in your daily life?

HEALING & INTEGRATION PROMPTS

41. Write about the scar, not the wound.
42. "I am learning to..." — Begin 7 sentences this way.
43. What part of you is ready to stop fighting?
44. Write about forgiveness without mentioning anyone else.

45. Complete: "Healing looks like..."
46. Describe the moment you chose yourself.
47. What are you integrating that you used to reject?
48. Write from the part of you that is already whole.
49. "I am not broken, I am..." — Finish it.
50. What does your future self want you to know?

FORM & CRAFT PROMPTS

51. Write a haiku about something ordinary that holds power.
52. Take a 10-line poem and reduce it to 5. What remains?
53. Write a sonnet about containment.
54. Create a villanelle using a phrase you repeat to yourself.
55. Write in someone else's voice, then translate it to yours.
56. Use only one-syllable words for an entire poem.
57. Write the same emotion in 3 different forms.
58. Create a call-and-response poem for community.
59. Write an erasure poem from a text that once governed you.
60. Build a poem where each line begins with the same word.

BODY & NERVOUS SYSTEM PROMPTS

61. Where does anxiety live in your body? Describe its shape.
62. Write from your breath, not your brain.
63. "My body knows..." — List 10 things it knows before your mind does.
64. What does safety feel like in your body?
65. Write about the moment your body said no and you listened.
66. Describe your heartbeat. Give it a voice.
67. What temperature is your grief?
68. Write about sensation without naming emotion.
69. "I feel it in my..." — Complete with 5 different body parts.
70. What does alignment feel like?

SOVEREIGNTY & AUTHORITY PROMPTS

71. Write 10 one-sentence truths you live by.

72. "I do not explain myself when..."

73. What law would you erase?

74. Write about power that doesn't dominate.

75. Complete: "I govern myself by..."

LINEAGE CONVERSATIONS

Dialogues Across Time with Black Writers and Revolutionary Voices

These conversations are not biographies. They are poetic dialogues— extending the insights of influential Black writers into contemporary practice. Each includes historical context, a Luxorae conversation poem, prompts, and a regulation practice.

JAMES BALDWIN — THE COST OF BELONGING

Who He Was & Why He Matters

James Baldwin was not merely a writer; he was a diagnostician of American identity. His work exposed the psychological cost of domination—not only to the oppressed, but to the oppressor. Baldwin understood earlier than most that racism was not primarily a moral failure, but an identity failure: a refusal to confront oneself honestly.

What makes Baldwin essential to a Luxorae framework is his refusal to sentimentalize either suffering or integration. He warned that belonging purchased through self-erasure is not liberation—it is a subtler captivity. His essays and novels return again and again to the same question: What does it cost a person to survive inside a lie?

Baldwin's authority came from clarity without hatred. He did not scream. He did not posture. He insisted on truth as an ethical obligation. That insistence is the foundation of internal sovereignty.

Luxorae Conversation Poem

Belonging is expensive
when it requires the disappearance of the self.
They call it peace
when you stop asking to be seen.
But I have learned—
any room that demands silence
charges rent in spirit.
I no longer bargain for safety
with my wholeness as collateral.

Guided Prompts

1. Where have you mistaken acceptance for safety?
2. Write a poem titled "Rent"—what does belonging cost you?
3. Where do you soften truth to remain welcome?
4. What would belonging look like without self-editing?

Regulation Practice

Boundary Statement (spoken aloud):
"I do not belong where I must abandon myself."

Key Terms
- **Authorship**: Choosing yourself without negotiation
- **Alignment**: Inner truth matching outer life
- **Luxury**: No self-erasure required for peace

LANGSTON HUGHES — THE DREAM WITHOUT BEGGING

Lineage Note

Langston Hughes restored dignity to ordinary Black life. He wrote in the language of people who were rarely treated as poetic subjects and insisted that dreams were not abstractions, but rightful expectations. Hughes refused to make aspiration polite.

His genius was accessibility without dilution. He understood that liberation required language people could carry, repeat, and believe. Dreams, for Hughes, were not wishes; they were signals of rightful life delayed by distortion.

Luxorae Conversation Poem

Dreams do not ask permission.
They dry up when life contradicts them.
If the dream is deferred,
it is not because it is foolish—
it is because something is leaking.
I do not beg for what agrees with me.

Guided Prompts

1. What dream have you been taught to downplay?
2. Write a poem using the word "table."
3. Where does your life contradict your longing?
4. What dream feels too big to speak aloud? Write it anyway.

Regulation Practice

Breath Practice:
Inhale for 4, exhale for 6.
Repeat until urgency leaves the body.

Key Terms

- **Luxury**: Space for desire without shame
- **Alignment**: Desire matched with structure
- **Source**: Trusting what you know you deserve

GWENDOLYN BROOKS — THE INTERIOR KINGDOM

Lineage Note
Gwendolyn Brooks dignified interior life. She showed that ordinary moments contain governance. Her work insists that sovereignty begins at home—not in grand gestures, but in quiet decisions.

Brooks wrote about kitchenettes, beauty parlors, and everyday Black life with the same rigor others reserved for "important" subjects. She proved that power lives in the mundane, and that how you organize your interior world is how you practice freedom.

Luxorae Conversation Poem
The kingdom was never distant.
It was waiting inside
quiet decisions.
Not the loud ones—
the small ones.
How I keep my space.
How I speak to myself.
How I refuse what does not align.

Guided Prompts
1. Write about an ordinary object that holds power for you.
2. Where does your sovereignty live quietly?
3. What interior habit governs your life?
4. Describe your "interior kingdom"—what does it look like?

Regulation Practice

Home Practice:
Order one small space intentionally today.
Notice how external order affects internal calm.

Key Terms

- **Governance**: Interior order
- **Luxury**: Peace at home
- **Sovereignty**: Power in the mundane

AUDRE LORDE — THE EROTIC AS LIFE FORCE

Lineage Note

Audre Lorde named the erotic as a source of power—not sexuality, but aliveness. She taught that intuition, pleasure, and depth were not indulgences but intelligence. Lorde matters because she restored trust in inner knowing.

She warned against living from disconnection, from numbness, from the flat safety of never feeling fully. The erotic, for Lorde, was the opposite of superficial—it was the deepest knowing, the body's yes before the mind approves.

For a full exploration of how Luxury of Poetry is in dialogue with Audre Lorde's 1980 essay "Poetry Is Not a Luxury," see "A Note on Lineage and Diaspora."

Luxorae Conversation Poem

They taught us to fear depth
because depth resists control.
But life-force is not reckless.
It is accurate.
I trust what knows before proof.
The body says yes
before the mind agrees—
that is not foolishness.
That is source.

Guided Prompts
1. Where have you distrusted pleasure?
2. Write "I knew before…" ten times. Finish each sentence.
3. What part of you is edited for safety?
4. Where does your body say yes that your mind wants to refuse?

Regulation Practice

Sensory Practice:
Name 3 things you enjoy without justification.
Let yourself feel pleasure for 60 seconds without explaining why.

Key Terms
- **Source**: Life-force intelligence
- **Alignment**: Trusting embodied knowing
- **Erotic**: Depth, not performance

CLAUDIA RANKINE — THE RECEIPT AND THE BODY

Lineage Note
Claudia Rankine exposes how harm operates through accumulation rather than spectacle. Her work reveals how the body stores microaggressions, tone, erasure, and policy as lived experience. She documents the quiet violence that shapes identity.

Rankine matters because she makes visible what systems try to normalize. She insists that psychological harm is real harm, and that recognition is the first act of liberation. She gives language to what we've been taught to dismiss.

Luxorae Conversation Poem
Some injuries arrive as tone.
Some as paperwork.
Some as silence that expects compliance.

My body remembers
what my mouth was trained to excuse.
Healing is not forgetting.
It is reclaiming authority while remembering accurately.

Guided Prompts

1. List three "receipts" your body carries.
2. Write in fragments—one line per incident.
3. Where have you minimized harm to remain composed?
4. What injury have you been told to "get over"? Write about it honestly.

Regulation Practice

Body Scan:

Name sensation without story for 2 minutes.
Where does your body hold what your mind dismissed?

Key Terms

- **Coherence**: Body and truth agreeing
- **Alignment**: No minimizing lived experience
- **Receipt**: Evidence the body keeps

JUNE JORDAN — TRUTH AS PUBLIC SERVICE

Lineage Note

June Jordan believed truth was a communal responsibility. Her work insisted that clarity was a form of care, and that silence could become complicity. She wrote as though language could protect life—because sometimes it did.

Jordan matters because she modeled what it means to speak not for attention, but for preservation. She understood that some truths must be told not because they're comfortable, but because lives depend on them being named.

Luxorae Conversation Poem

Clarity is not cruelty.
It is care without disguise.
If my voice saves nothing else,
let it save my integrity.
Some truths are not optional.
They are structural.
They hold the roof.

Guided Prompts

1. What truth do you soften unnecessarily?
2. Write a poem addressed to "You."
3. Where does silence cost you more than speech?
4. What truth are you responsible for speaking?

Regulation Practice

Alignment Statement:

"I speak what preserves dignity."
Say it aloud until your body believes it.

Key Terms

- **Authorship**: Stewardship of speech
  - **Alignment**: Truth lived, not argued
  - **Clarity**: Care without compromise

LUCILLE CLIFTON — SMALL POEM, HEAVY DOOR

Lineage Note

Lucille Clifton mastered precision. Her poems are minimal yet immense—proof that power does not require excess. She wrote from a place of acceptance that did not ask for permission, apology, or spectacle.

Clifton matters because she teaches restraint as authority. Her work models a sovereignty that is quiet, embodied, and complete. She showed that you can say everything in a few lines if the lines are true.

Luxorae Conversation Poem

I do not need many words
when the right ones hold weight.
Clean edges.
No leakage.
This is not smallness.
This is mastery.

Guided Prompts

1. Write a 6-line poem, then reduce it to 4.
2. Where can you remove excess in your life?
3. What boundary would sharpen your peace?
4. Practice saying no in 3 words or fewer.

Regulation Practice

Editing Practice:

Remove one unnecessary obligation today.
Notice the space it creates.

Key Terms

- **Luxury**: No unnecessary friction
- **Sovereignty**: Clean boundaries
- **Precision**: Mastery through less

AMIRI BARAKA — RUPTURE AND RESPONSIBILITY

Lineage Note

Amiri Baraka embodied rupture. His work shattered complacency and exposed rage as information. But rupture without regulation burns out movements. Baraka matters because he shows both the necessity and the danger of fire.

His legacy asks: What remains after the shout? What do you build when the anger cools? Baraka's work is a reminder that intensity can wake us, but sustainability requires something else.

Luxorae Conversation Poem

Fire wakes us.
But something must remain afterward.
I choose truth that builds
after the shout ends.
Rage is information—
not a lifestyle.

Guided Prompts

1. Write a poem titled "After the Fire."
2. Where does intensity replace sustainability?
3. What truth are you willing to live, not just declare?
4. Where does your rage point? What does it protect?

Regulation Practice

Pacing Practice:

Slow one decision today.
Feel the difference between urgency and importance.

Key Terms

- **Luxury**: Sustainability over spectacle
- **Alignment**: Power that lasts
- **Fire**: Energy that must be contained

STERLING A. BROWN — FOLK WISDOM AS AUTHORITY

Lineage Note
Sterling A. Brown preserved vernacular wisdom. He understood language as survival technology. He matters because he honored intelligence outside institutions—the knowing that lives in how people actually speak.

Brown refused to "elevate" Black vernacular into "proper" English. He insisted it was already whole, already authoritative, already enough. His work is a reminder that we do not need institutional approval to be intelligent.

Luxorae Conversation Poem
Our language carried us
before they called it improper.
Now I speak it whole.
No translation.
No apology.
No performance of palatability.

Guided Prompts
1. Write in your natural voice.
2. Where do you code-switch out of fear?
3. What wisdom did you inherit that wasn't in books?
4. What would it sound like to stop translating yourself?

Regulation Practice

Voice Practice:
Speak one truth without translation.
Use the words that come first, not the "correct" ones.

Key Terms
- **Authorship**: Naming yourself
- **Alignment**: Language without apology
- **Vernacular**: Intelligence as spoken

CLAUDE MCKAY — RAGE WITH FORM

Lineage Note
Claude McKay disciplined anger. He proved that rage could be shaped without dilution. His sonnets taught that form can sharpen resistance—that containment is not surrender, it is strategy.

McKay matters because he refused the false choice between feeling and structure. His work shows that intensity can be held, directed, and made precise without being diminished.

Luxorae Conversation Poem
They expect anger to sprawl.
I give it structure.
Containment turns fury
into direction.
The sonnet does not soften rage—
it sharpens it.

Guided Prompts
1. Write anger inside a strict form (sonnet, haiku, villanelle).
2. Where does discipline feel like safety?
3. What emotion needs structure?
4. How does restraint change what you're saying?

Regulation Practice

Containment Practice:
Hold silence for 30 seconds after emotion.
Let the feeling settle before you speak.

Key Terms
- **Form**: Mercy
- **Alignment**: Emotion governed, not erased
- **Discipline**: Strategy, not surrender

SONIA SANCHEZ — BREATH AS BLADE

Lineage Note
Sonia Sanchez fused discipline, spirituality, and political clarity. Her work shows that softness and strength are not opposites. She matters because she proved that breath can be as powerful as volume—that calm authority cuts deeper than shouting.

Sanchez's poetry is precise, rhythmic, and unflinching. She writes with the control of a master and the clarity of someone who knows exactly what she's saying. Her work is a lesson in power that doesn't leak.

Luxorae Conversation Poem
My voice does not rush.
It lands.
Breath makes truth unmovable.
I do not raise my voice
to be heard.
I lower it
until you have to listen.

Guided Prompts

1. Read your poem aloud.
2. Where does breath tighten?
3. What would slowness protect?
4. Rewrite something you shouted—say it in a whisper instead.

Regulation Practice

Breath Count:

Inhale 4, hold 2, exhale 6.
Repeat until your voice steadies.

Key Terms

- **Luxury**: Calm authority
- **Alignment**: Breath and truth together
- **Blade**: Precision that cuts

NIKKI GIOVANNI — REVOLUTIONARY TENDERNESS

Lineage Note

Nikki Giovanni proved that revolution does not require hardness. Her work celebrates Black joy, love, and tenderness as acts of resistance. She matters because she refused the narrative that strength must look stern.

Giovanni wrote about love, family, and everyday beauty with the same political clarity others reserved for protest. She showed that caring for yourself and your community is revolutionary work.

Luxorae Conversation Poem

Tenderness is not weakness.
It is refusal.
I will not harden
just because the world is hard.

Softness that survives
is the most dangerous thing.

Guided Prompts

1. Write about something you love without irony.
2. Where have you performed toughness to be taken seriously?
3. What part of you stays soft despite everything?
4. Write a love poem to yourself.

Regulation Practice

Tenderness Practice:

Do one gentle thing for yourself today.
Notice any resistance that arises.

Key Terms

- **Luxury**: Permission to be soft
- **Alignment**: Strength that doesn't harden
- **Tenderness**: Survival strategy

MAYA ANGELOU — RISING AS RESISTANCE

Lineage Note

Maya Angelou turned survival into ceremony. Her work insists that rising—again and again—is the ultimate act of defiance. She matters because she refused to let trauma have the final word.

Angelou's "Still I Rise" is not just a poem—it's a declaration that resilience is resistance. She showed that you don't have to justify your survival or explain your strength. You simply rise.

Luxorae Conversation Poem

They tried to bury me.
I chose to bloom anyway.

Rising is not forgiveness.
Rising is refusal.
I do not rise to prove anything.
I rise because I am still here.

Guided Prompts

1. Write about a time you rose when no one expected you to.
2. What keeps trying to bury you?
3. Complete: "Still I rise because…"
4. What does rising look like when no one is watching?

Regulation Practice

Rising Ritual:

Stand. Say aloud: "I am still here."
Feel your feet on the ground.

Key Terms

- **Resilience**: Refusal to stay down
- **Alignment**: Survival as defiance
- **Rising**: The body's yes to life

TONI MORRISON — LANGUAGE AS SOVEREIGNTY

Lineage Note

Toni Morrison understood that whoever controls language controls reality. Her work insists that naming is power, that storytelling is world-building, and that Black people have the right to define themselves.

Morrison matters because she refused to write for the white gaze. She wrote from and for Black people, trusting that universality comes from specificity. She showed that language is not neutral—it is sovereignty.

Luxorae Conversation Poem

I do not write to be understood
by those who refuse to see.
I write to build worlds
where I already belong.
Language is not decoration.
It is the architecture of reality.

Guided Prompts

1. What world are you building with your words?
2. Where do you write for approval instead of truth?
3. Who are you really writing for?
4. Write from your own gaze, not theirs.

Regulation Practice

Naming Practice:

Name yourself in your own words.
Not how others describe you—how you know yourself.

Key Terms

- **Sovereignty**: Self-definition
- **Authorship**: Building your own world
- **Language**: The power to name reality

COMPLETE GUIDE TO POETIC FORMS

Form as Containment, Not Constraint

This guide provides concise reference for major poetic forms. Each entry includes structure, purpose, and key elements.

FORM	STRUCTURE	PURPOSE
Sonnet	14 lines, rhyme scheme (ABABCDCDEFEFGG for Shakespearean)	Contains complex emotion through structure
Haiku	3 lines (5-7-5 syllables)	Captures single moment with precision
Villanelle	19 lines, 2 repeating refrains	Processes repetition and cycles
Pantoum	Repeating lines across stanzas	Weaves memory and present
Sestina	39 lines, 6 repeating end words	Deep pattern exploration
Ghazal	Couplets with repeating refrain	Spiritual longing and devotion
Free Verse	No fixed meter/rhyme	Natural speech patterns guide form
Prose Poetry	Poetic language in paragraph form	Lyric density without line breaks
Spoken Word	Performance-centered, oral delivery	Embodied voice and community

FORM	STRUCTURE	PURPOSE
Erasure Poetry	Removing words from existing text	Reclaiming authority from imposed language
Blues Poetry	AAB rhyme, call-and-response	Transformation through repetition
Praise Poetry	Direct naming and honor	Recognition of what endures
Lyric Essay	Hybrid of poetry and essay	Reflection with poetic language
Epigram	Brief, witty statement	Condensed truth or observation
Tanka	5 lines (5-7-5-7-7 syllables)	Extends haiku with reflection

Using Forms in Your Practice

- Start with the form that matches your need: containment (sonnet), processing (villanelle), precision (haiku)
- Don't force perfection—use structure as safety, not restriction
- Experiment with hybrid forms (sonnet + prose, haiku + free verse)
- Let form regulate your nervous system through predictable structure

THE LUXORAE POETRY PRACTICE

A 12-Week Liberation, Craft & Healing Curriculum

This curriculum can be used individually, in community, or as a facilitated circle. Each week includes a theme, form, liberation focus, practice, and reflection.

Week 1 — Voice Without Performance

- **Form:** Free Verse
- **Focus:** Speaking without impressing
- **Practice:** Write one poem you will never share
- **Reflection:** Where did your language soften when no one was watching?

Week 2 — Breath as Authority

- **Form:** Haiku
- **Focus:** Regulation & presence
- **Practice:** Write one haiku per day for 7 days
- **Reflection:** What changes when less is allowed?

Week 3 — Naming the Inheritance

- **Form:** Praise Poem
- **Focus:** Identity reclamation
- **Practice:** Write a praise poem for yourself without irony
- **Reflection:** What felt hardest to praise?

Week 4 — Containment

- **Form:** Sonnet
- **Focus:** Discipline as safety
- **Practice:** Hold a conflict inside the form
- **Reflection:** Did the structure calm or frustrate you?

Week 5 — Breaking Cycles
- **Form:** Villanelle
- **Focus:** Repetition & release
- **Practice:** Identify one inherited belief and write it into repetition
- **Reflection:** Where did the cycle loosen?

Week 6 — Diaspora Memory
- **Form:** Prose Poetry
- **Focus:** Ancestral voice
- **Practice:** Write from a memory that is not only yours
- **Reflection:** What did you carry that wasn't named before?

Week 7 — Silence as Wisdom
- **Form:** Erasure Poetry
- **Focus:** Authority without excess
- **Practice:** Erase a text that once governed you
- **Reflection:** What remained?

Week 8 — Anger Without Burnout
- **Form:** Spoken Word (written, not performed yet)
- **Focus:** Rage with containment
- **Practice:** Write without escalating volume
- **Reflection:** What happened when you didn't peak?

Week 9 — The Nervous System Speaks
- **Form:** Lyric Essay
- **Focus:** Body intelligence
- **Practice:** Write from sensation, not story
- **Reflection:** Where does your body hold truth?

Week 10 — Rewriting Authority
- **Form:** Epigram / Aphorism
- **Focus:** Condensed truth

- **Practice:** Write ten one-sentence truths you live by now
- **Reflection:** Which one feels non-negotiable?

Week 11 — Community Voice

- **Form:** Call-and-Response Poem
- **Focus:** Collective alignment
- **Practice:** Write a poem meant to be read aloud together
- **Reflection:** How does alignment change in community?

Week 12 — Occupancy

- **Form:** Your Choice
- **Focus:** Integration
- **Practice:** Write one poem that feels complete
- **Reflection:** What no longer feels urgent?

RHYTHM & PERFORMANCE GUIDE

The Luxorae Guide to Breath, Rhythm & Embodied Voice

Understanding Rhythm as Regulation

Rhythm is not just aesthetic—it is neurological. When you write or perform poetry with intentional rhythm, you are literally regulating your nervous system and the nervous systems of your listeners.

Why Rhythm Matters:

- Predictable patterns calm the amygdala (fear center)
- Repetition allows the brain to process difficult content safely
- Breath regulation through rhythm activates the parasympathetic nervous system
- Communal rhythm creates co-regulation (shared nervous system safety)

READING POETRY ALOUD: FOUNDATIONS

1. BREATH IS THE FOUNDATION

Practice:

- Place one hand on your chest, one on your belly
- Breathe so your belly expands first (diaphragmatic breathing)
- Inhale for 4 counts, exhale for 6
- This is your baseline breath before speaking

In Performance:
- Line breaks are breath cues
- Stanza breaks are deeper breath moments
- Don't rush through emotion—let breath hold it

2. PACING: SLOW DOWN
Most people read poetry too fast.

Practice:
- Read your poem at your normal pace
- Now cut that speed in half
- That's closer to the right pace

Why:
- Slowness allows meaning to land
- Pauses create emphasis
- Speed = anxiety; slowness = authority

3. VOLUME ≠ POWER
Common Mistake: Thinking louder = more powerful
Truth: Quiet, steady voice with clear articulation is more commanding than shouting

Practice:
- Whisper your most powerful line
- Notice how intensity doesn't require volume
- Use volume strategically, not constantly

PERFORMANCE VS. PRACTICE

PERFORMANCE:
- For audience

- Emphasis on delivery
- External validation
- Energy outward

PRACTICE:

- For self
- Emphasis on truth
- Internal alignment
- Energy inward

Both are valid. Know which you're doing.

EMBODIED PERFORMANCE TECHNIQUES

GROUNDING BEFORE YOU SPEAK

1. Feel your feet on the floor
2. Take 3 deep breaths
3. Locate your voice in your body (chest, throat, belly)
4. Speak from there, not from your head

USING YOUR BODY

Hands:

- Let them move naturally
- Use gesture to emphasize, not distract
- Still hands = grounded energy

Eyes:

- Memorize or be very familiar with your poem
- Make eye contact (if safe)
- Looking down = introspective; looking up = reaching

Stance:
- Feet shoulder-width apart
- Knees slightly bent (not locked)
- Weight evenly distributed
- This is literally grounding

CALL-AND-RESPONSE STRUCTURE

Traditional Format:
- Leader speaks a line
- Community responds
- Rhythm is co-created

How to Write for Call-and-Response:
1. Keep the "response" simple and repeatable
2. Build intensity through repetition
3. Let the community's voice amplify yours

Example:
Call: Who holds the power?
Response: We do.

Call: Who writes the story?
Response: We do.

Call: Who claims the future?
Response: We do.

BREATH PACING EXERCISES

EXERCISE 1: BREATH MAPPING
- Mark your poem with breath indicators:
- / = short breath

- // = long breath
- /// = pause for effect

EXERCISE 2: INHALE/EXHALE READING
- Inhale on punctuation
- Exhale through the line
- Notice how breath shapes meaning

EXERCISE 3: RHYTHM TAPPING
- Tap out the rhythm of your poem
- Find the pulse
- Let your voice follow that beat

RECORDING YOURSELF

Why Record:
- Hear yourself objectively
- Catch pacing issues
- Notice vocal patterns
- Track improvement

What to Listen For:
- Where do you rush?
- Where do you lose breath?
- What words get swallowed?
- Where does your voice crack or strain?

Adjust and re-record.

COMMUNITY WITNESSING PRACTICES
What is Witnessing: Holding space for someone's voice without judgment, correction, or performance critique.

How to Witness:
1. Listen with your whole body
2. Don't interrupt or "help"
3. Don't critique unless invited
4. Reflect back what you heard: "I heard... I felt... I noticed..."

Why it Matters: Being witnessed without judgment allows the nervous system to feel safe with voice.

PERFORMANCE ANXIETY REGULATION

Before Performing:
1. **Ground:** Feel your feet, breathe deep
2. **Remind yourself:** "I am not here to be perfect. I am here to be present."
3. **Reframe:** Performance anxiety and excitement feel the same in the body—choose to call it excitement

During Performance:
- If you lose your place: Pause. Breathe. Continue.
- If you get emotional: Let it be. Tears are not failure.
- If you forget a line: Say what's true in the moment

After Performing:
- Don't apologize for anything
- Receive feedback without defending
- Let the experience complete in your body (shake, stretch, breathe)

PRACTICE RITUALS

DAILY VOICE PRACTICE:
1. Speak one true sentence aloud every morning
2. Read one poem aloud (yours or someone else's)

3. Hum or tone to warm up your voice

WEEKLY SHARING PRACTICE:
- Share one poem with a trusted person
- No feedback required—just witnessing
- Notice how your voice changes when witnessed

RHYTHM AS RITUAL
Poetry is not just language.
It is rhythm made meaning.
It is breath made audible.
It is the body remembering how to be whole.
When you speak poetry aloud, you are not performing.
You are practicing sovereignty.

APPENDIX: THE SCIENCE OF POETRY & HEALING

How Poetry Regulates the Nervous System

THE NEUROSCIENCE OF WRITING & HEALING
Why Writing Helps (And Talking Sometimes Doesn't)

The Brain Under Trauma:
- Trauma lives in the **amygdala** (emotional center) and **hippocampus** (memory center)
- When traumatic memories activate, the **prefrontal cortex** (rational brain) goes offline
- This is why you can "know" something logically but still feel it emotionally

What Writing Does:
1. **Activates the prefrontal cortex** — Writing engages the thinking brain, which helps regulate emotion
2. **Creates narrative structure** — The brain processes experience more effectively when it has a beginning, middle, and end
3. **Provides distance** — Putting words on paper creates space between you and the experience
4. **Encodes memory differently** — Writing helps move trauma from "happening now" to "happened then"

Research: Dr. James Pennebaker's studies show that expressive writing improves immune function, reduces stress, and decreases symptoms of depression and PTSD. Writing about trauma for 15-20 minutes over 4 days shows measurable health benefits.

POLYVAGAL THEORY & POETRY

What is Polyvagal Theory?
Developed by Dr. Stephen Porges, polyvagal theory explains how the **vagus nerve** regulates our nervous system through three states:

1. **Ventral Vagal (Safe & Social)** — Calm, connected, regulated
2. **Sympathetic (Fight or Flight)** — Activated, anxious, survival mode
3. **Dorsal Vagal (Shutdown)** — Numb, frozen, dissociated

How Poetry Activates the Ventral Vagal State:
✓ **Rhythm** — Predictable rhythm signals safety to the nervous system
✓ **Breath** — Deep, paced breathing activates the vagus nerve
✓ **Prosody** — The musicality of language soothes the limbic system
✓ **Repetition** — Allows the brain to predict what comes next = safety
✓ **Witnessing** — Reading aloud to others activates social engagement system

In Practice:
• A sonnet's predictable structure = nervous system regulation
• A villanelle's repetition = trauma processing through safe return
• Spoken word's breath control = vagal tone activation

RHYTHM & BRAIN WAVES
How Rhythm Regulates the Brain
Brain Wave States:

• **Beta (12-30 Hz)** — Alert, thinking, problem-solving

- **Alpha (8-12 Hz)** — Relaxed, calm, creative
- **Theta (4-8 Hz)** — Meditative, deep relaxation
- **Delta (0.5-4 Hz)** — Deep sleep

What Poetry Does:
- Rhythmic reading/writing shifts brain from Beta → Alpha
- Repetitive forms (villanelle, pantoum) can reach Theta state
- This is the same state accessed through meditation and EMDR therapy

Why This Matters: When your brain is in Alpha/Theta, it can **reprocess trauma** without re-traumatizing.

THE POWER OF REPETITION

Why Villanelles, Pantoums & Blues Forms Heal

What Repetition Does:
1. **Desensitizes** — Repeated exposure to a difficult phrase reduces emotional charge
2. **Deepens** — Each return allows new meaning to emerge
3. **Integrates** — The brain processes in layers; repetition allows integration

Example: First time: "I learned to leave before I stayed." (Pain) Third time: "I learned to leave before I stayed." (Pattern recognition)

Sixth time: "I learned to leave before I stayed." (Understanding) Final time: "And then I didn't. That's how it changed." (Integration)

This is EMDR without a therapist.

EMBODIED COGNITION & POETRY

The Body Knows Before the Mind
Embodied Cognition Theory: The body holds knowledge that precedes conscious thought. Emotions are felt physically before they're understood mentally.

What This Means for Poetry:
- Writing from sensation ("My chest tightens") is more accurate than writing from concept ("I feel anxious")
- The body tells the truth when the mind lies
- Somatic poetry = accessing wisdom the thinking brain doesn't have access to

Practice: Instead of asking "What do I think about this?" Ask: "What does my body know about this?"

LANGUAGE SHAPES REALITY (LITERALLY)

Linguistic Relativity & Identity
The Sapir-Whorf Hypothesis: The language you use shapes how you perceive reality.

In Practice:
- Calling yourself "broken" vs. "healing" creates different neural pathways
- "I am angry" vs. "I feel anger" = different relationship to emotion
- Naming yourself accurately = claiming authority over your identity

Why the Luxorae Framework Emphasizes Naming:

- **Authorship** = naming yourself
- **Sovereignty** = defining your own terms
- **Alignment** = using language that matches internal truth

When you rename yourself, you rewire yourself.

FORM AS NERVOUS SYSTEM CONTAINER

Why Structure Isn't Restrictive—It's Regulatory

The Paradox of Form:

- Too much chaos = overwhelm
- Too much structure = rigidity
- Just-right structure = safety

How Forms Regulate:

Sonnet:

- 14 lines = manageable scope
- Rhyme scheme = predictable pattern
- Volta (turn) = space for shift
- Result: Complex emotion held safely

Haiku:

- 3 lines = extreme brevity
- No excess = precision
- Present moment only = grounding
- Result: Overwhelm reduced to essence

Free Verse:

- No imposed structure = freedom
- Self-imposed structure = agency

- Line breaks = choice points
- Result: Control without constraint

MIRROR NEURONS & WITNESSING

Why Being Heard Matters

Mirror Neurons: Brain cells that fire both when you act and when you observe someone else acting. This is the neurological basis of empathy.

What Happens When Someone Witnesses Your Poetry:
1. Their mirror neurons fire as if they're experiencing what you're saying
2. Your brain registers this as "being understood"
3. This activates the **ventral vagal (safe & social) system**
4. You feel seen without words

Why Community Circles Work: Co-regulation. Multiple nervous systems syncing up creates collective safety.

THE THERAPEUTIC SEQUENCE

How Poetry Moves Trauma Through the Body

Traditional Therapy Sequence:
1. Talk about the trauma
2. Process cognitively
3. Integrate emotionally
4. Move through the body

Poetry Sequence:
1. **Feel** it in the body (sensation)
2. **Name** it in language (writing)
3. **Contain** it in form (structure)
4. **Speak** it aloud (embodiment)

5. **Witness** it with others (integration)

Result: Trauma processed without re-traumatization.

NEUROPLASTICITY & PRACTICE

Why Repeating the Practice Rewires the Brain
Neuroplasticity: The brain's ability to form new neural pathways based on repeated experience.

What the 12-Week Practice Does:
- Week 1: New pathway forming (writing without performance)
- Week 4: Pathway strengthening (writing with containment)
- Week 8: Pathway becoming default (writing as regulation)
- Week 12: New baseline established (writing as sovereignty)

The Science: It takes **66 days on average** to form a new habit. The 12-week practice = 84 days = **new neural baseline**.

BREATHWORK & THE VAGUS NERVE

Why Breath-Focused Poetry Works
The Vagus Nerve: Runs from brainstem to abdomen, regulating heart rate, digestion, and emotional state.

How to Activate It:
- **Slow exhales** (longer than inhales) = vagal activation
- **Humming/toning** = direct vagal stimulation
- **Singing/chanting** = sustained vagal engagement

Poetry Techniques That Activate the Vagus:
- Reading aloud with paced breath
- Spoken word performance

- Chanting/repetitive forms
- Call-and-response (social engagement system)

Result: Regulated nervous system, reduced anxiety, increased resilience.

THE SCIENCE OF LUXURY AS INTERNAL ORDER

Why Internal Order = Nervous System Regulation

The *Luxury of Poetry* **Framework:** "Luxury is what does not press, leak, or require self-erasure."

The Neuroscience:
- **Press** = Chronic activation of sympathetic nervous system (stress response)
- **Leak** = Dysregulated boundaries, energy depletion
- **Self-erasure** = Disconnection from ventral vagal (safe self)

When you live with internal order (luxury):
- Parasympathetic nervous system is dominant (rest & digest)
- Cortisol levels decrease
- HRV (heart rate variability) improves = resilience
- Prefrontal cortex stays online = better decision-making

Luxury isn't indulgence. It's optimal nervous system function.

GLOSSARY OF LUXORAE TERMS

Alignment — Inner truth matching outer life; coherence between body and language

Authorship — Choosing yourself without negotiation; naming yourself

Coherence — Body and truth agreeing; integrated wholeness

Containment — Structure that holds without crushing; form as safety

Governance — Internal order and self-regulation

Luxury — Internal order; what does not press, leak, or require self-erasure

Occupancy — Presence without urgency; fullness without performance

Source — Life-force intelligence; what knows before proof

Sovereignty — Internal governance without external validation

Voice — Internal truth made audible; speaking from yourself

CONCLUSION
POETRY AS MEDICINE

Poetry works because it:
- ✓ Engages the thinking brain while processing emotion
- ✓ Provides structure that regulates the nervous system
- ✓ Uses rhythm to shift brain waves into healing states
- ✓ Activates the vagus nerve through breath and sound
- ✓ Creates safe containers for difficult truths
- ✓ Builds new neural pathways through repetition
- ✓ Allows witnessing without re-traumatization

This is not metaphorical healing.
This is measurable, neurological change.
Poetry is infrastructure.
And infrastructure practiced with internal order, spaciousness, and sovereignty?
That is luxury.

CLOSING WORD

This anthology is not meant to impress.
It is meant to hold.
Hold truth.
Hold breath.
Hold history.
Hold power without burning.
Poetry has always been how we stayed alive.
Now it can be how we stay whole.

References and Citations

This section provides academic, literary, and scientific sources that inform the Luxorae framework and the content of this book.

Primary Literary Sources

Works by the Black writers featured in the Lineage Conversations section:

Angelou, Maya. I Know Why the Caged Bird Sings. Random House, 1969.

Angelou, Maya. 'Still I Rise.' And Still I Rise: A Book of Poems. Random House, 1978.

Baldwin, James. The Fire Next Time. Dial Press, 1963.

Baldwin, James. Notes of a Native Son. Beacon Press, 1955.

Baraka, Amiri (LeRoi Jones). Black Magic: Collected Poetry 1961-1967. Bobbs-Merrill, 1969.

Brooks, Gwendolyn. A Street in Bronzeville. Harper & Brothers, 1945.

Brooks, Gwendolyn. Annie Allen. Harper & Brothers, 1949.

Brown, Sterling A. Southern Road. Harcourt, Brace and Company, 1932.

Clifton, Lucille. Good Woman: Poems and a Memoir 1969-1980. BOA Editions, 1987.

Giovanni, Nikki. Black Feeling, Black Talk, Black Judgment. William Morrow, 1970.

Hughes, Langston. The Weary Blues. Alfred A. Knopf, 1926.

Hughes, Langston. 'Harlem (Dream Deferred).' Montage of a Dream Deferred. Henry Holt, 1951.

Jordan, June. Some of Us Did Not Die: New and Selected Essays. Basic/ Civitas Books, 2002.

Lorde, Audre. 'Poetry Is Not a Luxury.' Sister Outsider: Essays and Speeches. Crossing Press, 1984, pp. 36-39.

Lorde, Audre. 'Uses of the Erotic: The Erotic as Power.' Sister Outsider: Essays and Speeches. Crossing Press, 1984, pp. 53-59.

Lorde, Audre. The First Cities. Poets Press, 1968.

McKay, Claude. Harlem Shadows: The Poems of Claude McKay. Harcourt, Brace and Company, 1922.

Morrison, Toni. Beloved. Alfred A. Knopf, 1987.

Morrison, Toni. Playing in the Dark: Whiteness and the Literary Imagination. Harvard University Press, 1992.

Rankine, Claudia. Citizen: An American Lyric. Graywolf Press, 2014.

Sanchez, Sonia. Shake Loose My Skin: New and Selected Poems. Beacon Press, 1999.

Neuroscience, Psychology, and Trauma Research

Scientific research supporting the therapeutic applications of poetry and expressive writing:

Pennebaker, James W. 'Writing About Emotional Experiences as a Therapeutic Process.' Psychological Science, vol. 8, no. 3, 1997, pp. 162-166.

Pennebaker, James W., and Joshua M. Smyth. Opening Up by Writing It Down: How Expressive Writing Improves Health and Eases Emotional Pain. 3rd ed., Guilford Press, 2016.

Porges, Stephen W. The Polyvagal Theory: Neurophysiological Foundations of Emotions, Attachment, Communication, and Self-Regulation. W.W. Norton & Company, 2011.

Porges, Stephen W. 'The Polyvagal Theory: New Insights into Adaptive Reactions of the Autonomic Nervous System.' Cleveland Clinic Journal of Medicine, vol. 76, Suppl 2, 2009, pp. S86-S90.

van der Kolk, Bessel A. The Body Keeps the Score: Brain, Mind, and Body in the Healing of Trauma. Viking, 2014.

Siegel, Daniel J. The Developing Mind: How Relationships and the Brain Interact to Shape Who We Are. 2nd ed., Guilford Press, 2012.

Shapiro, Francine. Eye Movement Desensitization and Reprocessing (EMDR) Therapy: Basic Principles, Protocols, and Procedures. 3rd ed., Guilford Press, 2018.

Levine, Peter A. Waking the Tiger: Healing Trauma. North Atlantic Books, 1997.

Dana, Deb. The Polyvagal Theory in Therapy: Engaging the Rhythm of Regulation. W.W. Norton & Company, 2018.

Cozolino, Louis. The Neuroscience of Psychotherapy: Healing the Social Brain. 3rd ed., W.W. Norton & Company, 2017.

Doidge, Norman. The Brain That Changes Itself: Stories of Personal Triumph from the Frontiers of Brain Science. Viking, 2007.

Frattaroli, Joanne. 'Experimental Disclosure and Its Moderators: A Meta-Analysis.' Psychological Bulletin, vol. 132, no. 6, 2006, pp. 823-865.

Smyth, Joshua M. 'Written Emotional Expression: Effect Sizes, Outcome Types, and Moderating Variables.' Journal of Consulting and Clinical Psychology, vol. 66, no. 1, 1998, pp. 174-184.

Embodied Cognition and Linguistic Theory

Research on the relationship between language, cognition, and bodily experience:

Lakoff, George, and Mark Johnson. Metaphors We Live By. University of Chicago Press, 1980.

Whorf, Benjamin Lee. Language, Thought, and Reality: Selected Writings of Benjamin Lee Whorf. Edited by John B. Carroll, MIT Press, 1956.

Varela, Francisco J., Evan Thompson, and Eleanor Rosch. The Embodied Mind: Cognitive Science and Human Experience. MIT Press, 1991.

Damasio, Antonio. Descartes' Error: Emotion, Reason, and the Human Brain. G.P. Putnam, 1994.

Gibson, James J. The Ecological Approach to Visual Perception. Houghton Mifflin, 1979.

Poetry Therapy and Expressive Arts

Clinical and therapeutic applications of poetry and creative writing:

Mazza, Nicholas. Poetry Therapy: Theory and Practice. 2nd ed., Routledge, 2016.

Fox, John. Poetic Medicine: The Healing Art of Poem-Making. TarcherPerigee, 1997.

Hynes, Arleen McCarty, and Mary Hynes-Berry. Biblio/Poetry Therapy—The Interactive Process: A Handbook. North Star Press, 1994.

Malchiodi, Cathy A., editor. Expressive Therapies. Guilford Press, 2005.

Adams, Kathleen. Journal to the Self: Twenty-Two Paths to Personal Growth. Warner Books, 1990.

Black Feminist Theory and Critical Race Studies

Theoretical frameworks informing the Luxorae approach to liberation and sovereignty:

hooks, bell. Feminist Theory: From Margin to Center. South End Press, 1984.

hooks, bell. Talking Back: Thinking Feminist, Thinking Black. South End Press, 1989.

Collins, Patricia Hill. Black Feminist Thought: Knowledge, Consciousness, and the Politics of Empowerment. Routledge, 1990.

Combahee River Collective. 'A Black Feminist Statement.' 1977. This Bridge Called My Back: Writings by Radical Women of Color, edited by Cherríe Moraga and Gloria Anzaldúa, Kitchen Table: Women of Color Press, 1981, pp. 210-218.

Crenshaw, Kimberlé. 'Mapping the Margins: Intersectionality, Identity Politics, and Violence against Women of Color.' Stanford Law Review, vol. 43, no. 6, 1991, pp. 1241-1299.

Taylor, Keeanga-Yamahtta. How We Get Free: Black Feminism and the Combahee River Collective. Haymarket Books, 2017.

Sharpe, Christina. In the Wake: On Blackness and Being. Duke University Press, 2016.

Hartman, Saidiya. Lose Your Mother: A Journey Along the Atlantic Slave Route. Farrar, Straus and Giroux, 2007.

African American Literary Criticism and History

Critical works on Black literary traditions and cultural production:

Gates, Henry Louis, Jr. The Signifying Monkey: A Theory of African-American Literary Criticism. Oxford University Press, 1988.

Baker, Houston A., Jr. Blues, Ideology, and Afro-American Literature: A Vernacular Theory. University of Chicago Press, 1984.

DuBois, W.E.B. The Souls of Black Folk. A.C. McClurg & Co., 1903.

Hurston, Zora Neale. 'Characteristics of Negro Expression.' Negro: An Anthology, edited by Nancy Cunard, 1934.

Neal, Larry. 'The Black Arts Movement.' The Drama Review, vol. 12, no. 4, 1968, pp. 28-39.

Bambara, Toni Cade, editor. The Black Woman: An Anthology. Washington Square Press, 1970.

Christian, Barbara. Black Feminist Criticism: Perspectives on Black Women Writers. Pergamon Press, 1985.

Poetic Form and Craft

Resources on poetic forms, techniques, and traditions:

Fussell, Paul. Poetic Meter and Poetic Form. Rev. ed., Random House, 1979.

Hirsch, Edward. A Poet's Glossary. Houghton Mifflin Harcourt, 2014.

Oliver, Mary. A Poetry Handbook. Harcourt Brace, 1994.

Strand, Mark, and Eavan Boland. The Making of a Poem: A Norton Anthology of Poetic Forms. W.W. Norton & Company, 2000.

Preminger, Alex, and T.V.F. Brogan, editors. The New Princeton Encyclopedia of Poetry and Poetics. 3rd ed., Princeton University Press, 1993.

Rhythm, Performance, and Oral Tradition

Works on the oral dimensions of African and African American poetic traditions:

Finnegan, Ruth. Oral Poetry: Its Nature, Significance and Social Context. Cambridge University Press, 1977.

Ong, Walter J. Orality and Literacy: The Technologizing of the Word. Methuen, 1982.

Smitherman, Geneva. Talkin and Testifyin: The Language of Black America. Houghton Mifflin, 1977.

Southern, Eileen. The Music of Black Americans: A History. 3rd ed., W.W. Norton & Company, 1997.

Floyd, Samuel A., Jr. The Power of Black Music: Interpreting Its History from Africa to the United States. Oxford University Press, 1995.

Additional References

Supplementary sources informing various aspects of this work:

Alexander, Michelle. The New Jim Crow: Mass Incarceration in the Age of Colorblindness. The New Press, 2010.

Brown, Brené. Daring Greatly: How the Courage to Be Vulnerable Transforms the Way We Live, Love, Parent, and Lead. Gotham Books, 2012.

Menakem, Resmaa. My Grandmother's Hands: Racialized Trauma and the Pathway to Mending Our Hearts and Bodies. Central Recovery Press, 2017.

Neff, Kristin. Self-Compassion: The Proven Power of Being Kind to Yourself. William Morrow, 2011.

Rosenberg, Marshall B. Nonviolent Communication: A Language of Life. 3rd ed., PuddleDancer Press, 2015.

Walker, Alice. In Search of Our Mothers' Gardens: Womanist Prose. Harcourt Brace Jovanovich, 1983.

Williams, Patricia J. The Alchemy of Race and Rights. Harvard University Press, 1991.

Online and Archival Resources

Digital archives and resources consulted for historical context:

Academy of American Poets. 'Learn About Poetry.' poets.org. Accessed January 2026.

The Poetry Foundation. 'Poetry Foundation Archive.' poetryfoundation. org. Accessed January 2026.

Schomburg Center for Research in Black Culture. 'Digital Collections.' New York Public Library, digitalcollections.nypl.org/collections. Accessed January 2026.

Library of Congress. 'The African American Odyssey: A Quest for Full Citizenship.' loc.gov/exhibits/odyssey. Accessed January 2026.

National Association for Poetry Therapy. napt.org. Accessed January 2026.

Permissions and Acknowledgments

All quoted material from published works is used in accordance with fair use provisions for criticism, commentary, and educational purposes. Brief excerpts from the following works appear in this book:

- Audre Lorde's 'Poetry Is Not a Luxury' (1977) - discussed and quoted in 'A Note on Lineage and Diaspora'
- Maya Angelou's 'Still I Rise' (1978) - referenced in lineage conversations
- Langston Hughes' 'Harlem (Dream Deferred)' (1951) - referenced in lineage conversations

Every effort has been made to trace copyright holders and to obtain their permission for the use of copyright material. The publisher apologizes for any errors or omissions and would be grateful if notified of any corrections.

A Note on Sources

This book draws on a wide range of academic, literary, and scientific sources to provide a comprehensive foundation for the Luxorae framework. The works cited represent foundational texts in Black literature, neuroscience, trauma therapy, embodied cognition, and poetry craft.

Readers seeking to deepen their understanding of any topic covered in this book are encouraged to consult the original sources listed in the References section.

For ongoing updates, additional resources, and community practice support, visit www.Luxoraelife.com

END OF LUXURY OF POETRY

About the Author

Luxorae is an author, poet, and community voice whose work centers on sovereignty, internal authority, and liberation through coherence. Luxorae is the creator of Luxorae™, a philosophical framework and applied body of work developed through rigorous study of scripture, philosophy, psychology, and formal academic training, and refined through lived experience and community engagement.

Educated in Buffalo, New York, Luxorae's work is rooted in both disciplined study and cultural proximity—bridging intellect with lived reality. Through writing, philosophy, and tangible offerings, Luxorae speaks to those who were taught how to survive, but never taught how to be free.

Luxorae's work does not offer escape or inspiration alone; it offers structure. Where systems demand compliance, Luxorae teaches alignment. Where institutions externalize power, Luxorae restores it inward. This work is grounded in love, culture, and collective elevation, serving as both a mirror and a blueprint for reclaiming internal authority.

Luxorae is not a symbol without substance. The work is authored, embodied, and lived—an architecture for freedom expressed through language, community, and practice.

Learn more at www.LuxoraeLife.com

www.ingramcontent.com/pod-product-compliance
Lightning Source LLC
Chambersburg PA
CBHW030635130626
46552CB00002B/863